Fabulous Fishes

Written and Illustrated by
Susan Stockdale

PEACHTREE
ATLANTA

For Jennifer, Janet, and Lulu,
with me every step of the way in creating this book
—*S. S.*

Special thanks to Dr. David Johnson of the National Museum of Natural History for his consistent, cheerful support and research assistance. Thanks also to Michelle Sattler and Mark Schick of the Shedd Aquarium and Jonelle Verdugo of the Monterey Bay Aquarium for their helpfulness.

Ω

Published by
PEACHTREE PUBLISHERS
1700 Chattahoochee Avenue
Atlanta, Georgia 30318-2112
www.peachtree-online.com

Text and illustrations © 2008 by Susan Stockdale

First trade paperback edition published in 2018

Art direction by Loraine M. Joyner
Typesetting by Melanie McMahon Ives

The illustrations were created in acrylic on paper.

Fish pictured on the endpapers: Front, left to right: fisher's angelfish, convict fish, Moorish Idol, eight-lined wrasse (Hawaiian reefs); Back, left to right: pennantfish, yellow-tail wrasse (Hawaiian reefs)

Printed in June 2018 by RR Donnelley & Sons in China
10 9 8 7 6 (hardcover)
10 9 8 7 6 5 4 3 2 1 (trade paperback)
10 9 8 7 6 5 (board book)

HC ISBN: 978-1-56145-429-7
PB ISBN: 978-1-68263-099-0
BB ISBN: 978-1-56145-637-6

Library of Congress Cataloging-in-Publication Data

Stockdale, Susan.
Fabulous fishes / written and illustrated by Susan Stockdale.
p. cm.
ISBN 978-1-56145-429-7
1. Fishes—Juvenile literature. I. Title.
QL617.2.S72 2008
597—dc22
2007029749

Round fish,

clownfish,

fish that like to hide.

Striped fish,

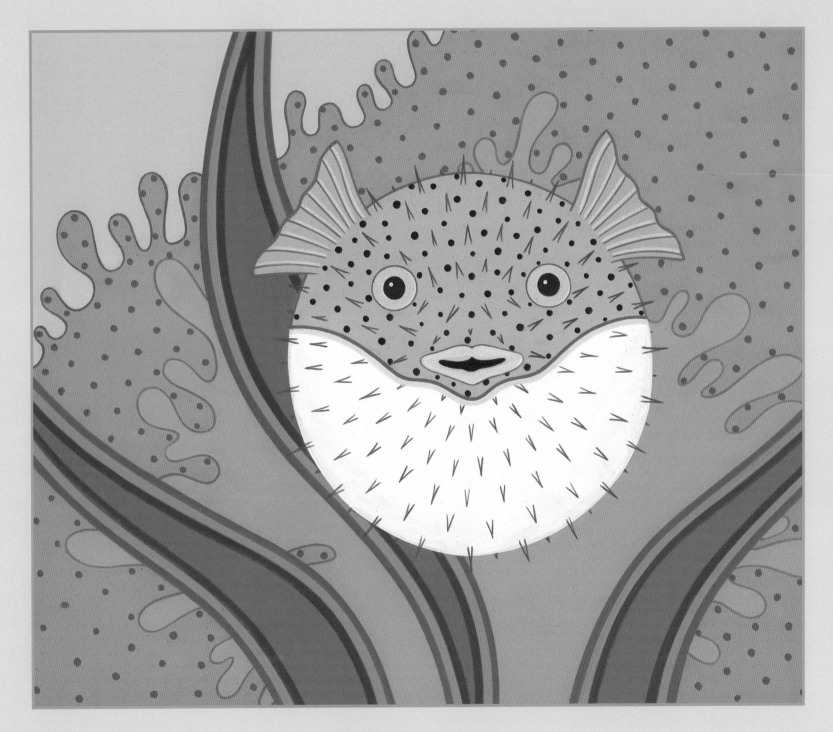

spiked fish,

fish that leap and glide.

Sand fish,

land fish,

fish that flash their lights.

Speckled fish,

spotted fish,

fish with tails curled tight.

Shiny fish,

spiny fish,

fish that hitch a ride.

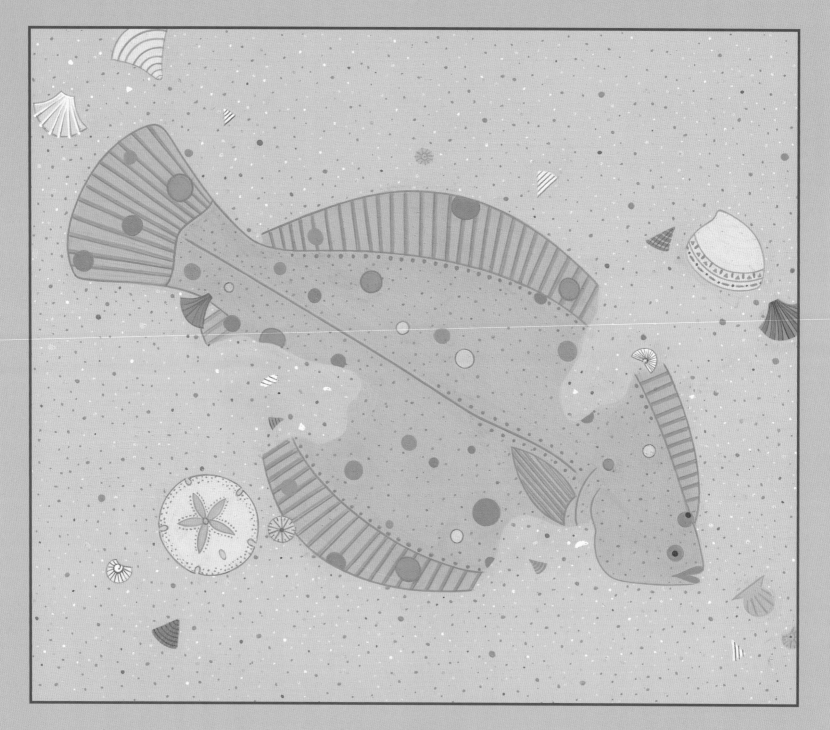

Flatfish,

catfish,

fish that ride the tide.

Fish that swim in numbers,

fish that swim alone.

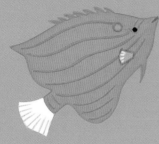

No matter what they look like,
they call the water home.

The **discus** is flat and round like a pancake, allowing it to swim easily among upright reeds. (Amazon basin)

The **flyingfish** bursts up out of the water, spread its fins, and glides through the air to escape larger fish. (Warm ocean waters worldwide)

The **clownfish** hides safely among the poisonous tentacles of sea anemones. It is protected from the poison by a slimy substance on its skin. (Pacific and Indian Oceans)

The **garden eel** retreats into its sandy sea burrow at the slightest alarm. (Oceans worldwide)

The **giant kelpfish** can change color to look like a piece of kelp. (Eastern Pacific Ocean)

The **mudskipper** use its front fins like little legs to pull itself up, skip along the muddy shore, and even climb trees. (Coastal mangrove forests and mudflats worldwide)

The **butterflyfish** uses its long, pointed snout to search the cracks of coral for tiny animals to eat. (Indian, Pacific, and Western and Eastern Central Atlantic Oceans)

Lanternfishes and **hatchetfishes** flash lights located along their sides to stay together in the deepest, darkest parts of the ocean. (Oceans worldwide)

When threatened, the **porcupine-fish** blows up like a spiky balloon so it will appear too large to fit into a predator's mouth. (Atlantic, Pacific, and Indian Oceans)

Every year, the **steelhead rainbow trout** travels from the salty ocean water to fresh water to lay its eggs. (Eastern Pacific Ocean, but widely introduced elsewhere)

The **bluespotted stingray** has stinging spines on its whiplike tail, which it uses to defend itself. (Oceans worldwide)

The **catfish** uses feelers on its face to search for food on the river bottom. (Freshwaters of all continents except the Antarctic, and many oceans worldwide)

The **seahorse** has a long tail like a monkey, which it uses to hold on to ocean plants. (Tropical coastal waters worldwide)

California grunions swim up on shore during high tide and bury their eggs on the sandy beach. (Pacific Ocean)

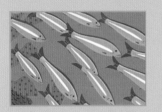

The silver bellies and sides of **sardines** help them blend with the shiny light from the sky, making them almost invisible to predators. (Oceans worldwide)

Bluestriped snappers travel in groups or "schools" to better defend themselves from predators. (Indo-Pacific Ocean)

When threatened, the **lionfish** turns the sharp, venomous spines on its back toward its enemies. (Indian, Pacific, and Western Atlantic Oceans)

The **swordfish** uses its long, sharp "bill" like a sword to kill other fishes. (Atlantic, Indian, and Pacific Oceans; the Mediterranean Sea; the Sea of Marmara; the Black Sea; and the Sea of Azov.)

Remoras attach themselves to a whale shark by suction disks on their heads, hitching a ride for miles and feeding on the shark's leftovers. (Oceans worldwide)

The bright yellow mouth of the **clown triggerfish** resembles that of a clown. (Indo-Pacific Ocean)

The **flounder** can adjust the colored markings on its flat, disc-shaped body to match the ocean floor. Its eyes are located on the same side of its head. (Oceans worldwide)

Also pictured on the last spread: **fairy basslets** (the orange fish is female and the multicolored fish is male); the **emperor angelfish** (yellow fish with blue stripes); and the **blueringed angelfish** (orange fish with blue stripes).

These are just a few of the many books I found helpful in developing the text and illustrations for FABULOUS FISHES:

ALL ABOUT SHARKS by Jim Arnosky (Scholastic)

CLASSIFYING FISH by Richard and Louise A. Spilsbury (Heinemann)

DISCOVERING SALTWATER FISH by Alwyne Wheeler (Franklin Watts)

NATIONAL AUDUBON SOCIETY FIRST FIELD GUIDE: FISHES by C. Lavett Smith (Scholastic)

FISH: A FIRST DISCOVERY BOOK edited by Sabine Krawczyk and Claude Delafosse (Scholastic)

FISH DO THE STRANGEST THINGS by Leonora and Arthur Hornblow (Random House)

FISHES: A GUIDE TO FRESH- AND SALT-WATER SPECIES by Herbert S. Zim and Hurst H. Shoemaker (St. Martins' Press)

FISHES: A TRUE BOOK by Melissa Stewart (Children's Press)

KILLER FISH by Russell Freedman (Holiday House)

RAYS: ANIMALS WITH AN ELECTRIC CHARGE by Andreu Llamas (Gareth Stevens Publishing)

SEA HORSES by Elaine Landau (Children's Press)

WHAT IS A FISH? by Lola M. Schaefer (Capstone Press)

WHAT IS A FISH? by Robert Snedden (Sierra Club Books)